FAITH'S
LITTLE INSTRUCTION
BOOK
Supercharged Quotes To Blast Doubt Out Of Your Life!

HARRISON HOUSE INC. · TULSA, OKLAHOMA

Faith's Little Instruction Book:
 Supercharged Quotes To Blast Doubt Out of Your Life!
ISBN 0-89274-728-5
Copyright © 1994 by Harrison House, Inc.
P.O. Box 35035
Tulsa, Oklahoma 74153

3rd Printing
Over 76,000 in Print

Introduction

Faith's Little Instruction Book is a unique collection of powerful, faith-building quotes from leading Spirit-filled men and women of past and present. These quotes, coupled with Scriptures, will strengthen and encourage you to stand firm and trust in the promises of God.

Filled with the power and the Spirit of the Charismatic movement and those who lead it, this little book will challenge you to do more than stand by and watch things happen. It will move you into action to put God's Word into practice in your life. These quotes will stir your spirit as you read from Smith Wigglesworth, Kenneth E. Hagin, Marilyn Hickey, Kenneth Copeland, Gloria Copeland, Frederick K.C. Price, John G. Lake, F.F. Bosworth, Lester Sumrall, and many others.

This book is a treasury of wisdom from some of the greatest people of faith in our times, but more importantly, it is a treasury of the timeless wisdom and guidance of the Bible. Faith's Little Instruction Book was designed to be a burst of hope and inspiration – we pray that it is in your life!

There is no limit to the inexhaustible power of God, and an "atom of faith" can blast a whole range of material mountains.

Howard Carter

...if you have faith the size of a mustard seed, you shall say to this mountain, "Move from here to there," and it shall move; and nothing shall be impossible to you.

Matthew 17:20 NAS

5

Faith is needed for the impossible, and you dare to act on the Word as though the impossible had become a possibility...a reality.

E.W. Kenyon

...The things which are impossible with men are possible with God.

Luke 18:27

6

Beloved, it is not our long prayers but our believing God that gets the answer.

John G. Lake

But when ye pray, use not vain repetitions, as the heathen do: for they think that they shall be heard for their much speaking. ...your Father knoweth what things ye have need of, before ye ask him.

Matthew 6:7

The greatest power that God has given to any individual is the power of prayer.

Kathryn Kuhlman

Pray all the time. Ask God for anything in line with the Holy Spirit's wishes.

Ephesians 6:18a,b
TLB

8

I can get more out
of God by believing
Him for one minute
than by shouting
at Him all night.

Smith Wigglesworth

*And whatever you
ask for in prayer,
having faith and
[really] believing,
you will receive.*

Matthew 21:22 AMP

9

Faith does not wait for the walls to fall down; faith shouts them down!

F.F. Bosworth

...the people shouted with a great shout, that the wall fell down... and they took the city.

Joshua 6:20

God's promise is as good as His presence.

Andrew Murray

Then said the Lord...You have seen well, for I am alert and active, watching over My word to perform it.

Jeremiah 1:12 AMP

Faith takes God
without any *ifs*.
If God says anything,
faith says,
"I believe it";
faith says, "Amen"
to it.

D.L. Moody

...but speak the word only, and my servant shall be healed. When Jesus heard it, he marvelled, and said to them that followed, Verily, I say unto you, I have not found so great faith....

Matthew 8:8,10

Prayer must become as natural as breathing. With such prayer, men defeat spiritual forces arrayed against them that no human means could overcome.

Gordon Lindsay

The weapons we fight with are not the weapons of the world. On the contrary, they have divine power to demolish strongholds.

2 Corinthians 10:4
NIV

Whether we like it or not, asking is the rule of the Kingdom.

Charles H. Spurgeon

Ask, and it shall be given you; seek, and ye shall find; knock, and it shall be opened unto you.

Luke 11:9

Faith changes hope into reality.

Kenneth E. Hagin

*That ye be...
followers of them
who through faith
and patience inherit
the promises.*

Hebrews 6:12

Faith is an eye that can see the invisible. Faith is an ear that hears what others do not hear. Faith is a hand that can touch the intangible.

Lester Sumrall

By faith he (Moses) forsook Egypt, not fearing the wrath of the king: for he endured, as seeing him who is invisible.

Hebrews 11:27

A doubter often prays for things he already possesses.

T.L. Osborn

Blessed be the God and Father of our Lord Jesus Christ, who hath blessed us with all spiritual blessings in heavenly places in Christ.

Ephesians 1:3

The important thing is not the size of your faith – it is the One behind your faith – God Himself.

Oral Roberts

As for God, his way is perfect; the word of the Lord is tried: he is a buckler to all them that trust in him.

2 Samuel 22:31

18

This book of the law shall not depart out of thy mouth; but thou shalt meditate therein day and night, that thou mayest observe to do according to all that is written therein: for then thou shalt make thy way prosperous, and then thou shalt have good success.

Joshua 1:8

When it comes to making major changes it's better to be too slow than too fast because it's easier to play catch up than clean up.

Buddy Harrison

I waited patiently for the Lord; he turned to me and heard my cry.

Psalm 40:1 NIV

Take a stand of faith and say, "Devil, you are a liar. I am going to believe God for a miracle because He is going to turn this situation around."

R.W. Schambach

Then Jesus answered and said unto her, O woman, great is thy faith: be it unto thee even as thou wilt. And her daughter was made whole from that very hour.

Matthew 15:28

Faith clamps down the teeth of God's Word on the seat of the enemy's pants and hangs on until Satan quits!

Marilyn Hickey

Therefore put on God's complete armor, that you may be able to resist and stand your ground on the evil day [of danger], and, having done all [the crisis demands], to stand [firmly in your place].

Ephesians 6:13 AMP

Dare to step across the faith line! A faith line is an irreversible decision to do the Word of God – to take a stand of faith. It's a line you draw when you need God to do the "impossible" in your life.

Kenneth Copeland

He staggered not at the promise of God through unbelief; but was strong in faith, giving glory to God.

Romans 4:20

There is no need to
pray the problem.
What we need to do is
zero in on the answer.
Pray and speak the
answer; cast the
problem over on Him.

Charles Capps

*Casting all your
care upon him; for
he careth for you.*

1 Peter 5:7

The God-kind of faith believes in the heart that what it says with the mouth will come to pass, and then dares to say it!

Frederick K.C. Price

...I believed, and therefore have I spoken; we also believe, and therefore speak.

2 Corinthians 4:13

25

The natural and the supernatural coming together make an explosive force for God.

Kenneth Hagin, Jr.

...faith by itself, if it is not accompanied by action, is dead.

James 2:17 NIV

When the power of God and faith are operative in your life, you are like a tank; you have the ability to move your position forward without taking any losses!

Rick Renner

With your help I can advance against a troop; with my God I can scale a wall.

2 Samuel 22:30 NIV

God does not give victory over the world just to a select few. He has given overcoming victory to every person that is born again.

Billy Joe Daugherty

For whatsoever is born of God overcometh the world: and this is the victory that overcometh the world, even our faith. Who is he that overcometh the world, but he that believeth that Jesus is the Son of God?

1 John 5:4,5

You'll never win a battle on the shells you fired in the last war. When a new enemy comes, it's time to reload.

Creflo A. Dollar, Jr.

So then faith cometh by hearing, and hearing by the word of God.

Romans 10:17

29

God channels all the power of heaven through the authority of the believer who knows the rights and privileges that belong to him and are found in the name of Jesus.

Bob Yandian

And on the basis of faith in His name, it is the name of Jesus which has strengthened this man whom you see and know; and the faith which comes through Him has given him this perfect health in the presence of you all.

Acts 3:16 NAS

When the storms of life strike, it's what happens "in" you that will determine what happens "to" you.

Jerry Savelle

I have set the Lord always before me: because he is at my right hand, I shall not be moved.

Psalm 16:8

I want to tell you something and don't ever forget it: if you're born again, you're a covenant child, and you've got rights, and what affects you affects God.

Dwight Thompson

And I will make my covenant between me and thee, and will multiply thee exceedingly.

Genesis 17:2

32

To become a champion in your walk with the Lord, you will go through a great battle. You will always live in victory, if you walk in the spirit and learn the way of the Spirit.

Pat Harrison

Therefore David ran, and stood upon the Philistine, and took his sword, and drew it out of the sheath thereof, and slew him, and cut off his head therewith. And when the Philistines saw their champion was dead, they fled.

1 Samuel 17:51

33

When you pray,
something is
happening to you!
It is not a myth;
it is the action of God.

John G. Lake

And when they had prayed, the place was shaken where they were assembled together; and they were all filled with the Holy Ghost, and they spake the word of God with boldness.

Acts 4:31

What is faith, you ask? Well,
it is an inner assurance that
the things we hope for actually
exist, and the conviction that
they are already ours even
though we cannot see them.

Hebrews 11:1 Lovett

Prayer has two pillars. Trust and Faith.

Charles Nieman

May the God of hope fill you with all joy and peace as you trust in him, so that you may overflow with hope by the power of the Holy Spirit.

Romans 15:13 NIV

One with God is a majority.

Billy Graham

If God be for us, who can be against us?

Romans 8:31b

37

Prayer is the key
in the hand of faith
which unlocks
heaven's storehouse.

*If my people, which
are called by my
name, shall humble
themselves, and
pray, and seek my
face, and turn from
their wicked ways;
then will I hear
from heaven,
and will forgive
their sin, and will
heal their land.*

2 Chronicles 7:14

This power does not work just as DYNAMITE to bring one explosive experience in your life. It is continual power!

John Osteen

But you shall receive power (ability, efficiency, and might) when the Holy Spirit has come upon you. . . .

Acts 1:8 AMP

Thinking faith thoughts and speaking faith words will lead your heart out of defeat and into victory.

Kenneth E. Hagin

...and this is the victory that has overcome the world – our faith.

1 John 5:4 NAS

Fear is the reverse gear of faith. Fear releases the ability of Satan against you. Faith releases the ability of God on your behalf.

Charles Capps

For God hath not given us the spirit of fear; but of power, and of love, and of a sound mind.

2 Timothy 1:7

41

Faith is not believing that God can, but that God *will*!

Jesus said...If thou canst believe, all things are possible to him that believeth.

Mark 9:23

Faith never rises above its confession.

E.W. Kenyon

From the fruit of his words a man shall be satisfied with good....

Proverbs 12:14 AMP

If we seek to feed
the fire of our prayers
with the fuel
of God's Word,
all our difficulties in
prayer will disappear.

R.A. Torrey

*Evening, and
morning, and at
noon, will I pray,
and cry aloud:
and he shall hear
my voice. He hath
delivered my soul
in peace....*

Psalm 55:17

It is time we circled the wagons, pulled out the artillery, rolled up our sleeves, and readied ourselves to be tough with the devil.

Rod Parsley

So give yourselves humbly to God. Resist the devil and he will flee from you.

James 4:7 TLB

45

Faith sings in your heart, no matter what assaults your soul.

Lester Sumrall

And now shall mine head be lifted up above mine enemies round about me: therefore will I offer in his tabernacle sacrifices of joy; I will sing, yea, I will sing praises unto the Lord.

Psalm 27:6

It's hard for God to walk with a man who gets *his* mind made up to do things his own way.

Norvel Hayes

Can two walk together, except they be agreed?

Amos 3:3

47

If you want to change your life, you have to change your confession.
The miracle is in your mouth.

John Osteen

The tongue has the power of life and death, and those who love it will eat its fruit.

Proverbs 18:21 NIV

48

We, all the while, gazing not on what is seen, but on what is unseen; for what is seen is transient, but what is unseen is imperishable.

2 Corinthians 4:18 Twentieth Century N.T.

Sometimes God doesn't tell us His plan because we wouldn't believe it anyway.

Carlton Pearson

...which ye will not believe, though it be told you.

Habakkuk 1:5

Be quick to repent and quick to forgive and you'll never be far from God.

Kenneth E. Hagin

And whenever you stand praying, forgive, if you have anything against anyone; so that your Father also who is in heaven may forgive you your transgressions.

Mark 11:25 NAS

51

You had better take time to pray until Jesus is glorified in your eyes; then you will be able to make Him glorious to others.

Aimee Semple McPherson

Let your light so shine before men, that they may see your good works, and glorify your Father which is in heaven.

Matthew 5:16

Let us not neglect prayer just because we do not fully comprehend the infinite power of the God at whose throne we kneel. I do not know everything about gravity, but I know it works.

Leroy Brownlow

The prayer of a righteous man is powerful and effective.

James 5:16b NIV

It is not the greatness of my faith that moves mountains, but my faith in the greatness of God.

...the exceeding greatness of his power to us-ward who believe, according to the working of his mighty power.

Ephesians 1:19

54

How very powerful the Word of God is! It has turned the course of history many times. It has guided conquerors and doomed infidels.

John Avanzini

For the word of God is quick, and powerful, and sharper than any two-edged sword, piercing even to the dividing asunder of soul and spirit, and of the joints and marrow, and is a discerner of the thoughts and intents of the heart.

Hebrews 4:12

When Satan brings
a worried thought
to your mind, tell him
to talk to God about
it. It's all in God's
hands, not yours.

Kenneth Copeland

*Therefore do not
worry and be
anxious....*

Matthew 6:31 AMP

56

By His (Jesus) *stripes ye were healed.* Your healing is already provided. You don't need to pray for it.

T.L. Osborn

...the punishment that brought us peace was upon him, and by his wounds we are healed.

Isaiah 53:5 NIV

57

You understand that there are two kinds of faith: Sense Knowledge faith that demands physical evidence to satisfy the senses...and the other kind of faith that depends upon the Word alone.

E.W. Kenyon

...blessed are they that have not seen, and yet have believed.

John 20:29

Our prayers lack power because we have not entered the realm of faith that fellowship alone will produce.

Dennis Burke

God is faithful, by whom ye were called unto the fellowship of his Son Jesus Christ our Lord.

1 Corinthians 1:9

59

...we can never have
more of true faith
than we have
of true humility.

Andrew Murray

*Humble yourselves
therefore under the
mighty hand of God,
that he may exalt
you in due time.*

1 Peter 5:6

It is by faith that we have to live, not by what we can actually see.

2 Corinthians 5:7 Barclay

With God,
go even over the sea;
without Him,
not over the threshold.

...With men it is impossible, but not with God: for with God all things are possible.

Mark 10:27

The income of God's Word is the outcome of a changed life.

Edwin Louis Cole

The entrance of thy words giveth light; it giveth understanding unto the simple.

Psalm 119:130

63

You are a child of destiny. God is orchestrating and ordaining your steps and your life – if you are yielded to Him.

Carlton Pearson

Even every one that is called by my name: for I have created him for my glory, I have formed him; yea, I have made him.

Isaiah 43:7

Ransomed men need no longer pause in fear to enter the Holy of Holies. God wills that we should push on into His presence and live our whole life there.

A.W. Tozer

Let us therefore come boldly unto the throne of grace, that we may obtain mercy, and find grace to help in time of need.

Hebrews 4:16

The anointing is not some mystical something out there. The anointing is the presence and power of God manifested.

Rodney Howard-Browne

The anointing which ye have ye need not that any man teach you. . . .

1 John 2:27

66

Payday doesn't come every Saturday night, but if you are faithful to God and His Word, payday always comes.

Oretha Hagin

O love the Lord, all ye his saints: for the Lord preserveth the faithful, and plentifully rewardeth the proud doer.

Psalm 31:23

Faith is not a sword just to grab...faith is a way of life.

Lester Sumrall

For therein is the righteousness of God revealed from faith to faith: as it is written, The just shall live by faith.

Romans 1:17

Faith in the devil is called *fear*.

Charles Capps

Leave no [such] room or foothold for the devil – give no opportunity to him.

Ephesians 4:27 AMP

69

Every day you make a choice: either you exercise faith and feast in the abundance of God's supply, or you give in to the devil and fear, and suffer personal famine.

John Avanzini

...choose you this day whom ye will serve....

Joshua 24:15

70

(Negative) thoughts are like birds, you can't keep them from flying around your head but you can keep them from building a nest in your hair.

Kenneth E. Hagin

Casting down imaginations, and every high thing that exalteth itself against the knowledge of God, and bringing into captivity every thought to the obedience of Christ.

2 Corinthians 10:5

Faith is the active
force which draws
the thin line between
success and failure.

Benson Idahosa

*For whatever is
born of God is
victorious over the
world; and this is
the victory that
conquers the world,
even our faith.*

1 John 5:4 AMP

72

Faith comes
by continually
considering Jesus.
Doubt comes
by considering
circumstances and
environment.

E.W. Kenyon

*...let us run with
endurance the race
that is set before us,
fixing our eyes on
Jesus, the author
and perfecter
of faith....*

Hebrews 12:2 NAS

73

Great victories come out of great battles.

Smith Wigglesworth

And having spoiled principalities and powers, he made a show of them openly, triumphing over them in it.

Colossians 2:15

Trust in the Lord with all your heart. Never rely on what you think you know.

Proverbs 3:5 Good News

Waiting is where the battle is won in the spiritual realm. Waiting and keeping our eyes on God. . . .

Joyce Meyer

I will say of the Lord, He is my refuge and my fortress: my God; in him will I trust.

Psalm 91:2

You need to be so full of the Holy Ghost that the devil knows who you are. God never intended for us to run away from the devil. God intended for us to run after him!

R.W. Schambach

Submit yourselves therefore to God. Resist the devil, and he will flee from you.

James 4:7

Faith opens the door
to God's promise
for you; and patience
keeps it open until
that promise
is fulfilled.

Kenneth Copeland

*Cast not away
therefore your
confidence,
which hath great
recompense of
reward. For ye have
need of patience,
that, after ye have
done the will of God,
ye might receive
the promise.*

Hebrews 10:35,36

Do not assume that
your faith is always
in top-notch shape!
Rather, play it safe
and assume that your
faith always needs
a fresh anointing!

Rick Renner

*...I shall be anointed
with fresh oil.*

Psalm 92:10

79

Faith and works should travel side by side, step answering to step, like the legs of men walking. First faith, and then works; and then faith again, and then works again —

until you can scarcely distinguish which is the one and which is the other.

William Booth

Even so faith, if it hath not works, is dead, being alone.

James 2:17

God is the great *I am*. *Am* is in the present tense. He is ready to do it now, so when you pray, believe that the promises of God are *yea* and *amen* in Christ Jesus.

Buddy Harrison

For no matter how many promises God has made, they are "Yes" in Christ. And so through him the "Amen" is spoken by us to the glory of God.

2 Corinthians 1:20
NIV

The result of prayer
in private will be
a life of boldness
and courage in public.

Edwin Louis Cole

*...and he continued
kneeling on his
knees three times
a day, praying and
giving thanks
before his God,
as he had been
doing previously.*

Daniel 6:10 NAS

83

You do not have the spirit of a quitter living inside you; you have the spirit of the only man in history to conquer death. You have the spirit of a winner – the spirit of Jesus Christ inside you.

Rod Parsley

The Spirit of him that raised up Jesus from the dead dwell in you. . . .

Romans 8:11

84

It is almost a sadness to my soul that men should be astonished and surprised at an ordinary, tangible evidence of the power of God.

John G. Lake

And He (Jesus) *marveled because of their unbelief – their lack of faith in Him.*

Mark 6:6 AMP

85

The whole difficulty is that we wish to pray in the Spirit and at the same time walk after the flesh. This is impossible!

Andrew Murray

For they that are after the flesh do mind the things of the flesh; but they that are after the Spirit the things of the Spirit.

Romans 8:5

Need is not what moves God; faith does. Vain repetitions do not move God; faith does. Much speaking does not move God; faith does.

Charles Capps

And without faith it is impossible to please Him, for he who comes to God must believe that He is, and that He is a rewarder of those who seek Him.

Hebrews 11:6 NAS

Fear knocked at the door. Faith answered and no one was there.

He will have no fear of bad news; his heart is steadfast, trusting in the Lord.

Psalm 112:7 NIV

"You see correctly," the Lord told me. "I'm watching over My word to make it come true."

Jeremiah 1:12 William F. Beck

He who moves mountains must make prayer a life habit.

Gordon Lindsay

Praying always with all prayer and supplication in the Spirit, and watching thereunto with all perseverance....

Ephesians 6:18

He can give only according to His might; therefore He always gives more than we ask for.

Martin Luther

...God will liberally supply (fill to the full) your every need according to His riches in glory in Christ Jesus.

Philippians 4:19
AMP

Real faith in God –
heart faith –
believes the Word
of God regardless
of what the physical
evidence may be.

Kenneth E. Hagin

I know what it is to be in need, and I know what it is to have plenty. I have learned the secret of being content in any and every situation....

Philippians 4:12 NIV

God's attitude is very plainly stated. He is a God of compassion and healing. Believe it and act upon it.

Roy Hicks

Beloved, I wish above all things that thou mayest prosper and be in health, even as thy soul prospereth.

3 John 2

93

Don't get bitter
or angry at God.
Fight the devil.
God wants you well.

Dodie Osteen

*The thief cometh
not, but for to steal,
and to kill, and to
destroy: I am come
that they might have
life, and that they
might have it more
abundantly.*

John 10:10

I have so much to
do that I must
spend several hours
in prayer before
I am able to do it.

John Wesley

*And when he
(Jesus) had sent
the multitudes
away, he went up
into a mountain
apart to pray....*

Matthew 14:23

95

To be possessed with an ever increasing faith one must make constant use of the faith that they have.

Charles S. Price

We ought and indeed are obligated [as those in debt] to give thanks always to God for you...because your faith is growing exceedingly....

2 Thessalonians 1:3
AMP

God has provided a power through the person of the Holy Spirit that will cause us to rise above our troubles.

Kathryn Kuhlman

But when He, the Spirit of truth, comes, He will guide you into all truth; for He will not speak on his own initiative, but whatever He hears, He will speak; and He will disclose to you what is to come.

John 16:13 NAS

97

We have good news for you! God will let you enjoy the supernatural!

John Osteen

Ye shall receive power, after that the Holy Ghost is come upon you. . . .

Acts 1:8

Prayer does not cause faith to work, faith causes prayer to work.

Gloria Copeland

...whatever you ask for in prayer, believe that you have received it, and it will be yours.

Mark 11:24 NIV

99

When I use the faith I have, God not only answers that but goes an extra step and gives things I could only imagine.

Bob Yandian

Now glory be to God who by his mighty power at work within us is able to do far more than we would ever dare to ask or even dream of – infinitely beyond our highest prayers, desires, thoughts, or hopes.

Ephesians 3:20 TLB

If we do not love one another we certainly shall not have much power with God in prayer.

D.L. Moody

The only thing that counts is faith expressing itself through love.

Galatians 5:6b NIV

Faith counts the thing done before God has acted.

Kenneth E. Hagin

Then they took away the stone from the place where the dead (Lazarus) was laid. And Jesus lifted up his eyes, and said, Father, I thank thee that thou hast heard me.

John 11:41

For no promise of God can fail to be fulfilled.

Luke 1:37 Phillips

Faith's possessions are just as real as physical possessions. Spiritual things are just as real as material things.

T.L. Osborn

Heaven and earth shall pass away, but my words shall not pass away.

Matthew 24:35

Take your faith and change what tomorrow brings.

Charles Capps

And as ye go, preach, saying, The kingdom of heaven is at hand. Heal the sick, cleanse the lepers, raise the dead, cast out devils. . . .

Matthew 4:24

105

Faith is a power that reams darkness.

Lester Sumrall

The people living in darkness have seen a great light; on those living in the land of the shadow of death a light has dawned.

Matthew 4:16 NIV

Faith keeps itself occupied only with His omnipotence.

Andrew Murray

...for the Lord God omnipotent reigneth.

Revelations 19:6

107

Faith-chilling items have nothing to do with the Christ of Pentecost. Whatever He touches catches fire.

Reinhard Bonnke

John answered, saying unto them all, I indeed baptize you with water; but one mightier than I cometh...he shall baptize you with the Holy Ghost and with fire.

Luke 3:16

108

Absorb the principle that failure is never final, so if you do not succeed the first time, keep on trying.

Daisy Osborn

Brethren, I count not myself to have apprehended: but this one thing I do, forgetting those things which are behind, and reaching forth unto those things which are before, I press toward the mark for the prize of the high calling of God in Christ Jesus.

Philippians 3:13,14

The human spirit,
once stretched by
an adventure of faith,
will never return
to its original size.

*For by You I can
run through a troop,
and by my God I
can leap over a wall.*

Psalm 18:29 AMP

If you want to receive blessings by the bushel load, start going to the Word with a bushel basket.

Kenneth Copeland

And he said unto them, Take heed what ye hear: with what measure ye mete, it shall be measured to you: and unto you that hear shall more be given.

Mark 4:24

111

God wants his people hot. He wants them growing and moving. He wants them striving for the best and pressing on.

Casey Treat

I count not myself to have apprehended: but this one thing I do, forgetting those things which are behind, and reaching forth unto those things which are before, I press toward the mark for the prize of the high calling of God in Christ Jesus.

Philippians 3:13,14

Heaven doesn't come to earth cheap. It never has! It takes prayer.

Norvel Hayes

The earnest (heartfelt, continued) prayer of a righteous man makes tremendous power available – dynamic in its working.

James 5:16b AMP

113

Faith cannot grow in the atmosphere of condemnation.

E.W. Kenyon

There is therefore now no condemnation to them which are in Christ Jesus, who walk not after the flesh, but after the Spirit.

Romans 8:1

The simplest soul can touch God and live in the very presence of God and in His power.

John G. Lake

...power belongeth unto God.

Psalm 62:11

We don't serve a dead God. We don't serve a God who has no power. Our God is still God.

Rodney Howard-Browne

Look unto me, and be ye saved, all the ends of the earth: for I am God, and there is none else.

Isaiah 45:22

...for which reason I assure you, that what things soever you pray for, if you believe that you shall obtain them, they shall be yours.

Mark 11:24 Alexander Campbell

You cannot go by what everything looks like. You have to go by what God's Word says and trust God. If you cannot trust God, who can you trust?

Happy Caldwell

Trust in the Lord with all thine heart: and lean not unto thine own understanding.

Proverbs 3:5

The Bible is true, no matter how vehemently some people try to deny or prove it wrong; it is God speaking to us, and it will work if you apply it to your life.

Ray McCauley

But be ye doers of the word, and not hearers only. . . .

James 1:22

119

Christians are not the hunted, but the hunters; not the attacked, but the attackers. We are God's storm troops, sent to release the hostages of hell.

Reinhard Bonnke

Ye are of God, Little Children, and have overcome them: because greater is he that is in you, than he that is in the world.

1 John 4:4

The secret of having more faith is to know more about God.

Lester Sumrall

That I may know him, and the power of his resurrection....

Philippians 3:10

Jesus taught His disciples not how to preach, only how to pray.

Andrew Murray

...one of his disciples said unto him, Lord, teach us to pray, as John also taught his disciples.

Luke 11:1

Child of God, the time for playing church is over, the King of kings and the Lord of lords is on His way back. The key to surviving and even thriving in this unprecedented era is knowing how to operate in faith.

Creflo A. Dollar, Jr.

Be on your guard; stand firm in the faith; be men of courage; be strong.

1 Corinthians 16:13
NIV

123

Only he who can see
the invisible can do
the impossible.

*...With men this
is impossible;
but with God all
things are possible.*

Mark 19:26

124

When we are in the Spirit we are unconquerable, invulnerable, going from victory to victory, our life hid with Christ in God.

Reinhard Bonnke

Now thanks be unto God, which always causeth us to triumph in Christ....

2 Corinthians 2:14

Don't dig up in doubt what you plant in faith.

And these are they which are sown among thorns; such as hear the word, and the cares of this world, and the deceitfulness of riches, and the lusts of other things enter in, choke the word, and it becometh unfruitful.

Mark 4:18,19

126

Some people wonder why they can't have faith for healing. They feed their body three hot meals a day and their spirit one cold snack a week.

F.F. Bosworth

...desire the sincere milk of the word, that ye may grow thereby.

1 Peter 2:2

Faith asks for no evidence other than the written Word of God.

Gloria Copeland

Now faith is being sure of what we hope for and certain of what we do not see.

Hebrews 11:1 NIV

It is in the quiet times in His presence worshiping, waiting, praising, and listening that you enter the highest levels of prayer.

Dennis Burke

I wait for the Lord, my soul doth wait, and in his word do I put my hope.

Psalm 130:5

Wishing will never be a substitute for prayer.

Edwin Louis Cole

You want what you don't have.... And yet the reason you don't have what you want is that you don't ask God for it.

James 4:2 TLB

130

Faith is the radar that sees through the fog.

Corrie ten Boom

Now faith is an assurance of things hoped for, a sure persuasion of things not seen.

Hebrews 11:1
Worrell N.T.

God has decreed
to act in response
to prayer. "Ask,"
He commands us.
And Satan trembles
for fear we will.

Ruth Bell Graham

*You can get
anything –
anything you ask
for in prayer –
if you believe.*

Matthew 21:22 TLB

But do you, dear friends,
build up your characters
on the foundation of your most
holy Faith, pray under the
guidance of the Holy Spirit.

Jude 20 Twentieth Century N.T.

It seems God is limited by our prayer life – that He can do nothing for humanity unless someone asks Him.

John Wesley

If you ask any thing in my name, I will do it.

John 14:14

Faith is in the
present tense.
It believes NOW.
It receives NOW.
It acts NOW.

Billy Joe Daugherty

Now faith is....

Hebrews 11:1

The more attention and weight you give the Word, the more revelation and power you're going to receive.

Creflo A. Dollar, Jr.

And when you draw close to God, God will draw close to you.

James 4:8a TLB

Marvelous victories have been won, then have been lost through "loose talk" – words spoken that were not needed.

T.L. Osborn

Don't talk so much. You keep putting your foot in your mouth. Be sensible and turn off the flow!

Proverbs 10:19 TLB

Exercising our faith and walking in the victory of God is sometimes hard, through some of the hardest tests that we have God has a way of leading us into a deeper place with Himself.

Pat Harrison

That the trial of your faith, being much more precious than of gold that perisheth, though it be tried with fire, might be found unto praise and honour and glory at the appearing of Jesus Christ.

1 Peter 1:7

If we expect to accomplish great things, then we must maintain constant communication and fellowship with God.

Jerry Savelle

Through Jesus, therefore, let us continually offer to God a sacrifice of praise – the fruit of lips that confess his name.

Hebrews 13:15 NIV

Do not worry or fret that God has given more faith to others than He has given to you. Rest assured in the fact that God has imparted enough faith to you to make sure you are covered from head to toe!

Rick Renner

...God hath dealt to every man the measure of faith.

Romans 12:3

You can believe all day long that the Bible is true – and that's to your credit – but what the Bible says will never affect your life in a personal way until you start acting on God's Word.

Frederick K.C. Price

Do not merely listen to the word, and so deceive yourselves. Do what it says.

James 1:22 NIV

Confession is to your faith as *thrust* is to an airplane.

Charles Capps

We boldly say what we believe [trusting God to care for us]....

2 Corinthians 4:13
TLB

Bulldog faith hangs
on to God's Word
until our enemy
is defeated and
our circumstances
are conquered.

Marilyn Hickey

*...being fully
persuaded that,
what he (God) had
promised, he was
able also to perform.*

Romans 4:21

The laws of nature
are positively altered
by the working
of miracles.

Howard Carter

*And the man of God
said, Where fell it?
And he showed him
the place. And he cut
down a stick,
and cast it in
thither; and the
iron did swim.*

2 Kings 6:6

144

For I assure you, whoever says to this mountain, "Be taken up and thrown into the sea!" and entertains no inner doubt, but believes that what he says will happen, it shall be so for him.

Mark 11:23 Berkeley

Your mind doesn't stay renewed anymore than your hair stays combed.

Kenneth E. Hagin

And be not conformed to this world: but be ye transformed by the renewing of your mind....

Romans 12:2a

Faith accepts no compromise. Faith knows no arbitration. Faith knows only superb fulfillment.

Lester Sumrall

Now the just shall live by faith: but if any man draw back, my soul shall have no pleasure in him.

Hebrews 10:38

(Jesus has) given us all authority and power to stomp on sin and sickness and every other demonic thing in the earth! Put the works of Satan under your feet....

Kenneth Copeland

And hath put all things under his (Jesus') feet, and gave him to be the head over all things to the church. Which is his body, the fullness of him that filleth all in all.

Ephesians 1:22,23

148

God is looking for men and women who will stand on His Word believing that if He said it, He will do it, and that if He spoke it, He will bring it to pass.

R.W. Schambach

And blessed is she that believed: for there shall be a performance of those things which were told her from the Lord.

Luke 1:45

149

What is the secret of prayer? What is the secret of moving mountains by the prayer of faith? The first thing is to recognize the presence of Him who created the mountains.

Gordon Lindsay

For by him were all things created, that are in heaven, and that are in earth, visible and invisible, whether they be thrones, or dominions, or principalities, or powers: all things were created by him, and for him.

Colossians 1:16

150

If we undertake to pray for a thing, then we ought either to follow it up until we get the answer or withdraw the petition.

F.F. Bosworth

Ask, and you will be given what you ask for. Seek, and you will find. Knock, and the door will be opened. For everyone who asks, receives. Anyone who seeks, finds. If only you will knock, the door will open.

Matthew 7:7,8 AMP

A little faith will bring your soul to heaven; a great faith will bring heaven to your soul.

Charles Spurgeon

And the peace of God, which passeth all understanding, shall keep your hearts and minds through Christ Jesus.

Philippians 4:7

I am not moved by what I see. I am not moved by what I feel. I am moved only by what I believe.

Smith Wigglesworth

Our life is lived by faith. We do not live by what we see in front of us.

2 Corinthians 5:7
New Life

153

Whenever we find the presence of the Holy Spirit, we will always find the supernatural.

Kathryn Kuhlman

But ye shall receive power, after that the Holy Ghost is come upon you: and ye shall be witnesses unto me... and unto the uttermost part of the earth.

Acts 1:8

154

Quit sweating, quit wrestling. It is not TRY but TRUST.

John G. Lake

Be careful for nothing; but in every thing by prayer and supplication with thanksgiving let your requests be made known unto God. And the peace of God, which passeth all understanding, shall keep your hearts and min/ through Chris/ Philippians/

When the spirit is
in perfect fellowship
with the Lord,
faith is as natural
as breathing.

E.W. Kenyon

*If you remain in
me and my words
remain in you,
ask whatever you
wish, and it will
be given you.*

John 15:7 NIV

A Psalm of Praise

But you'll arise with a freshness of heart,
and you'll realize then that the Spirit of God is not
going to depart.
But He will sustain you and keep you by His power
because you're about to enter into your finest hour,
the finest hour for the Church to sing,
the finest hour to worship the King,
the finest hour to overcome,
the finest hour because the victory is already won.

Buddy Harrison

References

Unless otherwise indicated, all Scripture quotations are taken from the *King James Version* of the Bible.

Scripture quotations marked NIV are taken from the *Holy Bible, New International Version* ®. NIV ®. Copyright © 1973, 1978, 1984 by International Bible Society. Used by permission of Zondervan Publishing House. All rights reserved.

Scripture quotations marked AMP are taken from *The Amplified Bible. Old Testament* copyright © 1965, 1987 by Zondervan Corporation. *New Testament* copyright © 1958, 1987 by the Lockman Foundation. Used by permission.

Verses marked TLB are taken from *The Living Bible*, copyright © 1971. Used by permission of Tyndale House Publishers, Inc., Wheaton, Illinois 60189. All rights reserved.

Scripture quotations marked NAS are taken from the *New American Standard Bible*. Copyright © The Lockman Foundation 1960, 1962, 1963, 1968, 1971, 1972, 1973, 1975, 1977. Used by permission.

The Twentieth Century New Testament, text by Wescott and Hort. Copyright © 1904, Fleming H. Revell Co., New York.

Scripture quotation marked George Campbell are taken from *The Sacred Writings of the Apostles and Evangelists of Jesus Christ*. Copyright © 1974, Gospel Advocate Co., Nashville.

The Worrell New Testament. Copyright © 1904, 1980, Gospel Publishing House. Springfield, MO.